University of Central Florida Contemporary Poetry Series

University Press of Florida / State University System

Florida A&M University, Tallahassee

Florida Atlantic University, Boca Raton

Florida Gulf Coast University, Ft. Myers

Florida International University, Miami

Florida State University, Tallahassee

University of Central Florida, Orlando

University of Florida, Gainesville

University of North Florida, Jacksonville

University of South Florida, Tampa

University of West Florida, Pensacola

University Press of Florida
Gainesville
Tallahassee
Tampa
Boca Raton
Pensacola
Orlando
Miami
Jacksonville
Ft. Myers

DIRT
EATERS

Teri Youmans Grimm

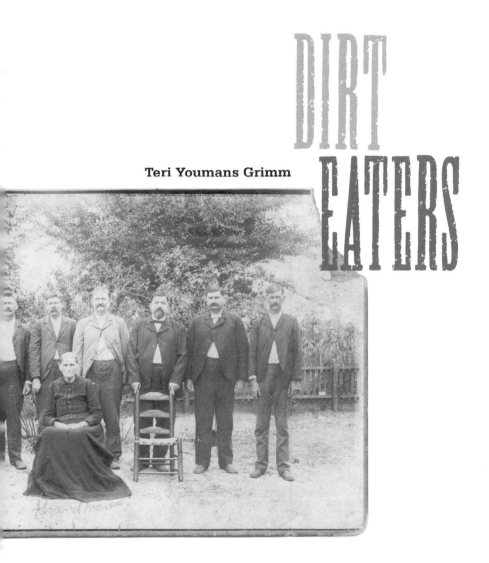

Parts of the following songs appear in this book:
"Will You Miss Me When I'm Gone?" by A. P. Carter
Copyright 1935 by Peer International Corporation
Copyright Renewed. International Copyrights Secured
All Rights Reserved. Used by Permission.
"When the World's on Fire" by A. P. Carter
Copyright 1930 by Peer International Corporation
Copyright Renewed. International Copyrights Secured
All Rights Reserved. Used by Permission.
"The Sun of the Soul" by A. P. Carter, Maybelle Carter, and Sara Carter
Copyright 1935 by Peer International Corporation
Copyright Renewed. International Copyrights Secured
All Rights Reserved. Used by Permission.

All photographs in text courtesy of the author.

Library of Congress Cataloging-in-Publication Data
Grimm, Teri Youmans.
Dirt eaters / Teri Youmans Grimm.
p. cm. — (University of Central Florida contemporary poetry series)
ISBN 0-8130-2723-3 (cloth: alk. paper) — ISBN 0-8130-2724-1 (pbk.: alk. paper)
I. Title. II. Contemporary poetry series (Orlando, Fla.)
PS3607.R564D47   2004
811'.6—DC22   2003070507

The University Press of Florida is the scholarly publishing agency for the State
University System of Florida, comprising Florida A&M University, Florida Atlantic
University, Florida Gulf Coast University, Florida International University, Florida
State University, University of Central Florida, University of Florida, University of
North Florida, University of South Florida, and University of West Florida.

University Press of Florida
15 Northwest 15th Street
Gainesville, FL 32611-2079
http://www.upf.com

For my father, G. B. Youmans Jr.,
who wanted me to always remember "who I am."

And especially for my husband, Chad,
who loves me in spite of it.

Contents

Acknowledgments

Grateful acknowledgment is made to the editors of the following publications, in which these poems first appeared (sometimes in earlier versions): *Baybury Review*, "Accountability"; *Connecticut Review*, "Dissipation"; *Drexel's On-line Journal (DOJ)*, "Mayport, 1975" and "Proverbs 16:33"; *The 2002 Emily Dickinson Awards Anthology*, "Anointed"; *Hurricane Alice*, "Ambrosia"; *Indiana Review*, "Consanguinity, Doc Youmans, Emmanuel County, 1908"; *The Journal* (Ohio State University), "Bestridden"; *Kalliope*, "The Anole"; *Nebraska Review*, "Down South Vapors," "Visitation," and "Dirt Eaters"; *Sierra Nevada Review*, "Mark 16:17–18"; *THEMA*, "John 9:39."

I am grateful to the Nebraska Arts Council for a grant which enabled me to complete this work.

Many thanks to Richard Duggin, Art Homer, Mark Cox, David Rivard, David Wojahn, Robin Behn, Frank Shimerdla, David Jauss, Sally Molini, Mary Helen Stefaniak, and Susan Aizenberg for all they've taught me about making poems.

— **Dirt Eaters**

Don't you want to go to Heaven

When the world's on fire?

Don't you want God's bosom

To be your pillow?

—A. P. Carter

Like a lapidary
with a jackhammer,
the delicate escapes me—so
the prairie seems
only simpering,
and the plains distal
compared to
alligators
in ditches, skunk
cabbage odor,
cottonmouths
sunning themselves
on the Buick,
an aunt who bit
a neighbor
for stealing figs.
I have cast
my laments out
on the St. Johns—
behold them aglow
like Spanish moss
shawls over aging
limbs, immutable
as the manners
of the place. They glow
like tungsten wire
hammered into luminance.
That brackish river
sidles over my tongue
so often, the alluvia
taste like tin.
Call it pining,
but it's a punishment

by degrees, this ancestral
conspiracy, it commands me
back, where my dead
will pin what they
want to on me. They pretend
to be such docile
ghosts, but I smell
their yellow breath.
They turn
roadkill into purses
and combs. They turn
roadkill into soft-
shell cooter soup.

Curled on the cool metal
lid of the washing machine,
cottonmouths were common as cats
that year. Mama grew leery of laundry,
wouldn't step into the utility room
without a hatchet. In the yard Daddy hacked
seven and damned the dried-up ditch
behind our house. August we all blistered
with fear. The Word didn't *live* inside of me yet
so summer long I wore dresses, pedaled
the neighborhood, Good News
Bible in my grip witnessed
to men changing oil, smoking
teenagers outside the Jiffy Mart,
any friends who'd risk
being seen with me, ladies
swinging toddlers.
Didn't they dread
the seven-headed beast, his ten-horned
blasphemies shouldering up through the earth?
Who wouldn't tremble to find their name
missing in the book of life
or hurled into the lake
of fire and glass clutch terror falling?
I pored over Revelation like tea leaves
from the top of the monkey bars—Christ's
little diviner! Seeing everything!
The end of the world began
in the cracked dirt below.
I shuddered each time a cloud passed
the sun. Like somebody opened
an umbrella in my soul, what if the sky
was dark with sanctified bodies—the shadow

passing in a blinking—and Heaven
was sealed off from me forever?
Through the screen
door I watched a severed
four-footer twirl around Daddy's leg.
One more sign.

Bits of white fire like nasty bugs
buzz around his tattooed arms,
land in his curly hair.

I am seven.

Through my bedroom window, Mr. Dixon welds
a race car on his carport. *CRAZY 8* painted on the side,
but it's not the game I play.

His wife—she's shown up
naked at our sliding
glass door, black eye, broken
teeth, more than once.
He doesn't flinch,

but I do when he holds the blowtorch
flame right beneath his forearm.
The hair shines but won't catch,
no blisters even. From here

I know his skin is cool
shade to touch because his eyes, turned
toward my window, are Aunt Deebie warm
like when she's in the Spirit.

I pay attention so I know things.

Aunt Deebie steals
perfume testers off Walgreen's
counter, Granddaddy hides dirty
magazines in his shed, and even

Thomas put his whole fist
inside Jesus's wound before he would believe.

The fire out, he sits in a lawn chair
drinking beer and later he'll go inside, maybe
punch his wife around like nothing
ever happened.

I drag my feet across the shag carpet,
touch the bed's metal frame.
What comes out of me is lit blue.
Like a wet cap, it hardly pops at all.

All of us watched, the mama too, as firemen
carried out three bodies, covered small mouths

with their own, as if they believed
life could be shouted back into them. The firemen

listened hard, rocking softly like praying,
but the kids, I knew, wouldn't say a word.

New Year's Eve, the house around the corner
stung our eyes and throats. *Drunk. Her and her boyfriend*

there, both cockeyed drunk, a voice spit near me. *Navy wife*,
my Daddy added as if it explained everything.

I thought of their daddy standing lonely watch on
the *Saratoga's* bow. I wondered if his gull-white uniform, glowing

faint like a candle, was any comfort
in the dark or if at this moment he remembered

how much the ship weighed,
how deep the ocean ran.

In baby-doll pajamas she swayed. It hurt,
watching her hand shudder a cigarette

to her mouth, ash poised over her bare feet.
She knelt among the small bodies.

All that was left
were embers, smoke, a burned out pool table,

charred sofa frame, a highchair, fused
plastic stack of 8-track tapes.

Wind feasted on the rest, smeared
my window black, then shifted out to sea.

Midway

The way I imagine it, skies over her
Maryland were always gray as the mullet
my Granddaddy quit work each spring to catch,
and Mama in a chenille robe stands at a window,

eyes trained on the horizon for Daddy's return
from the Zone-A-Light chemical plant. Other times
she's sitting at the kitchen table, licking the weekly Green
Stamps from the A&P, placing them

evenly in the book, hoping to get herself
a sewing machine or hand mixer.
Under the same
fish-dismal sky, Omaha wearies me.

A kind of missing
that becomes winter afternoons,
when closing my eyes I still can't remember
if the camellia shrubs in Grandma's yard

were red or white or how
they looked in full bloom, loneliness
in love that takes you away from an ocean
or swamp you understand, to a prairie.

On the phone Mama explains it wasn't like that
for her. She says the truth is important and I should
tell it honest because it's *her* story. From a small
bathroom window Mama could see the stars,

Tony Curtis, Kim Novak, Hope Lange on any given Friday
night at the Midway Drive-In just yards away
from the toilet where she sat in her pink chenille robe.
The ends of her hair still dripping from the bath

and doesn't she smell of plain, white soap?
With her knees tucked under her chin she has the best seat
in the house. On this particular Friday night, my Daddy out
of town inspecting plants in Ohio, she admires

Elizabeth Taylor's satin slip of sin. Lounging on a sofa,
Paul Newman holds whiskey in one hand, a crutch
in the other. Never mind Mama can't hear,
faint breezes coming off the verandah carry gardenias,

fragrant and soft as that slip and all the liquor in the delta
can't fix what's broken in the man. She's satisfied
in that bathroom, her neck two hours stiff
from tilting, cold night through an open window.

She says years later she saw the movie
on TV and though the small screen couldn't hold
half of Taylor's grace or the blue-depth of Newman's
eyes, it was just as she remembered. But what if she got it

wrong, if it was the kitchen window instead?
And not *Cat on a Hot Tin Roof* but *Vertigo*?
So what if Daddy was really sprawled in the next room
reading *Life* magazine or her robe was polished cotton?

It's how it felt, rising like warm air through the receiver,
my mother's voice in waves over the plains and everything
just as we remembered it, every word.
All of our regrets played out in one lump sum of hours.

Miss Senior High Duval County

I wore it as if Bill
Blass himself stitched it
just for me—it was
the only way, this dress,
my sister's five-year-old
chiffon and pink polyester
bridesmaid. No stylish pouf
at the bottom, but folds
at the bustline and the haltered
way it fastened around
my neck gave
the appearance of my having
more than I ever would.

Hidden between Missy's $300
powdered sugar confection
and Angie's lime hoopskirt
replete with lace and matching
sherbet parasol, I heard Missy whisper:
Pretty on the inside won't cut it here.

I heard it in thick letters, the black
Pull sign on a glass door
I pushed anyway,
as another patch of dollarweed
taking over the lawn.
I heard it in the dispossessed
hush of all those rubber bands
on a doorknob, the twist
ties in the back of a drawer.
As if I would ever run
out of means to hold things together.

But Saved is Saved
whether in alligator pumps

or dirty bare feet, my Grandma
said. So I tossed a slight tilt
of my head toward judges and a Look-
we-all-know-this-dress-is-a-hand-
me-down-but-isn't-the-excess-a-little-
silly-and-don't-you-love-the-way-I-rise-
above-it smile. It was the clincher.

Grandma's style was Debutante Circle.
A single-wide trailer—I learned early on
            a girl with shiny teeth boasting
            a cardiologist daddy
            and a dirt road that ends where it begins
            are not the same thing.

The added-on screened-in porch,
tobacco cans spilling
asparagus fern and jasmine. Chinaberries,
mimosas staggering
the yard. The way
it was,
was the only way.

Trophy clutched in my hands,
tiara hunkered smug
on my head,
I still wanted to ask her:
            How do you *always* look
            them eye to eye?
            To what account is it ever enough?
            When will a Circle stop
            being a circle,
            the dust rising up to greet me?

What Does It Matter

to his nurse Marie—placing a pillow
beneath my father's feet, exchanging
used sputum cups for new—
that a long dead uncle was appointed first
governor of South Carolina, owned a sugar
plantation in Barbados? But my father says it,
pride swelling like a wave in his voice.
In Marie's head the image might be her own
suffering, cramped in a splintered,
waterlogged boat
from Haiti to Florida's two bedroom
apartment and a rent-to-own TV.
He brought slaves
over with him, even let them live right
there in the house until their quarters were built.
This letting go of his hand is the only power
I have, the only distance between me
and where his story is going.
Across the room, my sister, Cheri, thumbs through
a magazine as if she hasn't heard
a thing. Even when we were young
she seemed able
to shield herself from his words,
her face never betraying
itself except to the pillow, smothering
the sound. And if I resent that ability,
it's because it isn't enough.
Not for a boy who parked his bike in front
of our cinder-block house. He wasn't even in the yard
but on the easement, throwing sticks and rocks
into the storm drain, just to see
the splash and swish beneath him.
Behind a post, I stood on the porch
with my father as he yelled for him to "Stop,

and God Almighty you better listen
to me, boy." But the kid,
still throwing stones, hunched over the drain,
ignored him, not like Cheri
pretending to hear, eyes wide open, head
tilted to one side—but outright disobeyed,
refused to turn around.
I could make myself look better here,
leave out the moment when I recognized
the boy, knew that he was deaf.
I said nothing before
my father grabbed him by the shoulders,
the kid so frightened he made a bellowing noise,
an open and hollow sound like a wounded cub.
He didn't hear you! He can't hear you!
But the words stayed in my mouth,
because my voice carried
across the lawn would be
shouting to the neighborhood
how wrong he was. When he figured it out,
this is what my father did: He didn't smooth
the boy's hair, or cup his face and say
with his eyes and mouth, *I'm sorry.*
He pulled his hands away
as though the boy were scalding metal,
then went inside, letting the screen door slap.
The boy crying and ashamed for no reason.
He's sorry, he really is.
I wanted to say it for all of us,
but I stood there on the porch
hugging the post, words lodged in my throat,
a stupid ambassador in a dangerous country
knowing only the words for *yes, please, more.*

Accountability

At nine I was a gutted fish,
standing in front of the congregation.
Emptied of all the great and terrible

sins that were mine. Flesh, I believed,
was tainted for saying *gosh* and *jeez*
when everyone knew you were taking

the Lord's name in vain. Corrupted
to the core for afternoons I stared
at pictures of naked statues, paintings

racy with bodies, parts I tried to draw
over and over, never getting them right.
Defiled by the words *I hate.*

I wanted to be like Peter, I thought
Jesus loved him best. Appeared first
to him on Easter and put him in charge

of the others. If I believed
He brought Lazarus back, made his chest rise
with life, fed the multitudes with five

loaves and fewer fish, if I knew
He walked on water all calm
after raising his arms—then what

else could I do but purge myself
out loud. Become a fisher of men. All
afternoon I looked to the sky,

waited for my confirmation,
a sign that said, *This is my own
daughter with whom I am well pleased.*

Friends, slumber is the underbelly of waking.
　　　Dreams slithered in, promptings urgent
beneath my door, sealed in vermilion
　　　wax. All acquiescent frailty, obeying
the first voice that breathed my name, the same
　　　voice of the devil, incessant. I'd been warned
he'd try to find me by people in the know:
　　　gardenia-laced Sunday school matrons
with crosses on their ears, around their necks
　　　like charms; dark half-moons
waned below Pastor's eyes, testament
　　　to vigilance. But, Brothers
and Sisters, in the deepest hours
　　　Saved is not enough to save me
from the tinny waltz that knells when I plummet
　　　through dream's trapdoor, the ballerina
on the music box—gilded splendor! Twirling
　　　atop a spiral staircase—no parapet
to hinder me, a pirouette descending
　　　into the devil's arms. Red velvet, marble,
mahogany, gilt—all out of time—swirl past
　　　until the room is eclipsed by the gyre
we dance in. Oh, Believers, forgive me
　　　when I confess I stand with him on the pinnacle
of that temple, throw myself off,
　　　indifferent to Christ—angels charging
beneath me before I wake to panic,
　　　dizzy-sick girl, smell of burnt
licorice seething my head, afraid of tumbling
　　　through the sky all I may have lost.
Sleepy children, the devil steals his way in
　　　where he can. To say I KNEW him

would be a lie, I never saw his face, but I can
        tell you he wears a gray worsted suit—
a lily in the buttonhole.

I do not know much
of martyrdom, what it's for
giving in to the voice
of Christ or wind.
I've touched the garments
of the zealots
and felt golden. But the fullness
passed when they went,
and I gathered doubt then
to seal those spaces
where cold seeped in.

Because I do not wholly
believe, each morning I wake
there's a hair on my pillow.
Each day a different
color—blonde, auburn, silver,
black. Not my own, but from
the scalps of others
like me. I pretend it isn't so.
My days are numbered, every strand
on my head
is numbered.

When these lips shall nevermore

Press a kiss upon thy brow,

But lie cold and still in death

Will you love me then as now?

—A. P. Carter

I put the gray sweater in my closet & today
I pulled it out because it was Tuesday & the dog was fed
& my work was done & no one was waiting for me
anywhere. Just as you expect, I held it to my face
& breathed him in so deeply it was suffocating.
Is it curious the way I choked on it? The smell,
my father's smell, that now belongs to me alone? It was 4:00
in the afternoon & I had no place to go.

Consanguinity

1. Doc Youmans, Emmanuel County, 1908

August clay dried to dust and mottling
corn, butterbeans and peanuts, turning them the
red of stung eyes, the eyes of cow and hog.

They say that summer
it seemed nothing
could make you take a breath,
like you'd already choked on Georgia dirt.

You were born neither
out of hope, nor desperation,
something in between, say, a debt
no one ever really counts on collecting.
Fourteenth child, naming you
after the doctor, Green Bell,
was a weary gesture. Even
the day's nomenclature
overwrought.

They say that summer
it was so bad
you were delivered freckled
in dust, like red pepper—no, chiggers—
eating you up.

2. A Teacher Writes a Letter to My Grandfather Regarding My Great Aunt Nannie Jane, 1924 (and What She May Have Had to Say about It)

Green Bell, I had a long trip and surely
was tired. Before I got home
I had a puncture and it just
raining the hardest kind.

Will you please see if you can find that
small razor strap of mine and send it to me?

Has Nannie Jane come back yet?
I know you will be kinder
ashamed to look at her at first sight,
for it seemed to get you
when we would mention it.

> *No fatted calf waiting*
> *on the spit, but here*
> *I am anyway. A breathing reminder*
> *of your greatest wish and fear.*
> *As though I'm some cripple*
> *in the street or a bearded woman,*
> *your eyes shun me. You only look*
> *when you think I'm not. Gape at me,*
> *you'll know I've seen things you've*
> *never even held pictures of.*
> *In the ocean so far, Georgia*
> *wasn't a speck of dirt, and the water*
> *turning exquisite blue*
> *as the delft bowl Mama never used.*
> *Still, without a sextant*
> *or a star, I could point dead-on the*
> *direction of our dog-trot*
> *house. Leaving didn't change*
> *who I am, it made me certain.*
> *But in departure you may lose*
> *your desire to return, Doc,*
> *you might discover how easy it is*
> *forgetting who you are—isn't*
> *that what makes you grind*

your teeth so hard
at night it sounds like milling corn?

Tell her to work hard this summer and plan
now to go to school every day this next term;
I would rather she take up
any other habit than loafing.
If there is anybody I don't want
to see be just an ordinary dollar or two
dollar worker 'tis her.

P.S. It's hanging there
on my bed I suspect. If you will
do that for me I will surely thank you
and do as much for you some time.

Out there, the water appeared
crawdad shallow, I thought I could
run my fingers along the depths just
by leaning over. Holding onto
the ladder, I eased myself in,
kicked my feet around and—nothing.
I knew how big the Atlantic was
then, that it could swallow me
whole. My lungs filled,
I would sink
like an open jar. Looking
up—the white, white hull—
and thinking, I can touch it,
I really can. Last object
I'd ever lay eyes on,
last thought,
last chance.

3. Screwball Comedy, 1934

He wipes a hand on his pant leg and blames the Royal
Palm Cola bottle sweat instead of her nearness. A ring
sits heavy as a hammer in his pocket and he shifts a little
from the heft of it. Above his head the smoke of a hun-
dred cigarettes lingers in the projection light like a va-
porous net. He hardly notices Claudette Colbert's heart-
shaped face, Gable's shockingly bare chest. He doesn't
know that next to him his girl (almost his wife, really)
is at this moment wondering if her face isn't the same
shape as the movie star's. *It Happened One Night*, she
knows that this will be part of the story she tells her son
and granddaughters, when they ask how he proposed.
Because she has suspected he might, she borrowed a
dress for the evening—blue sateen with a white Peter
Pan collar. Down to her patent leather pumps, her Avon
cologne, her rhinestone pin in the shape of a peacock,
she will remember. What she won't tell them, however,
is how he smells of swamp mud from working in the
Okefenokee for the CCC, as if he grew out of the dirt, so
present the odor is even on his breath. She overlooks it
for his tallness and the way his forearms bulged when he
helped her daddy fix the roof on the porch last Saturday.
Neither cares that outside the theater 4.7 million families
(to which they both belong) are on relief according to
the government or that Huey Long has announced his
"Every Man a King" wealth distribution plan, or that von
Hindenburg will die and Hitler will soon be president,
or that men's underwear sales will slump because Gable
wears no undershirt in the film. All that matters to him
is that her hair is so shiny and black, he swears he can see
his face in each strand. All that matters to her is that he
notices because she washed her hair in mayonnaise just

for this effect. This is real happiness. Two people in a
little smoke-filled theater in Waycross swept up in a his-
tory that hasn't happened yet. Walking toward the
Sunnyside Café they will see a shooting star and each will
make the same wish. Later that night when a meteorite
crashes in Arizona killing thirty-three head of cattle, and
dust storms in the west begin to blow 300 million tons of
topsoil into the Atlantic, and a few days later when Clyde
Barrow and Bonnie Parker are plugged fifty times for the
twelve lives they've taken and five days after that when
the Dionne Quintuplets are born in Canada—how would
you tell this couple their happiness will buckle under all
that weight? How would you ever find the words to tell
them, walking arm in arm past the dime store, toward the
fountain in the center of town where he will bend down
on one knee, her small hand in his much bigger one, *the
world is so much greater than the two of you.* How would you
ever find the words to tell them this?

4. For Crackers

*It's just our way of doing that bothers
some kinds,* Granddaddy told the police
who showed up at the neighbor's
behest. The engine lolled from the chinaberry tree
for a week, like the carcass of a boar

gutted then dismissed. He'd sold his Sinclair
station for better pay and insurance at Georgia Paper,
then repined his choice. The ulcer he considered his
due and poured more gravy on his dinner. *It's just our way*

to trade the witch for the devil. I loathe that sentence
handed down to me as though my only choice
is between evils. It's sewn in red above my chest,

like on his coveralls. Like his Bugler Boy tobacco, it emanates
from my skin. Like the cancer he called a consequence
of breathing, the words roost like buzzards—*It's just our way.*

5. Camera Lucida

The first picture I go to
in the albums, always—Grandma's black hair
combed rather than tortured
into occasion. Nearly disguised
without glasses and his hearing aid headband,
Granddaddy's naked young face.
They lie across a bed,
look straight at me in a way that hints
I never really knew them. I can only stare
back so long, knowing how it all turns out.

I pore over albums searching for these
little wounds and I find them everywhere:

> Here—Uncle Seward dressed in
> Aunt Nannie's clothes, another,
> (should I even mention it?) in blackface.

> Aunt Sula on the swinging bridge,
> Grandfather Mountain in July. The sweater
> hides the burn scar
> no one ever talked about.

> Daddy—a little boy in an aviator cap
> squats in a tobacco field. Bags
> filled dark beneath his already worried eyes.

If photography is a kind of resurrection
what about those memories that root around in darkness?
Revival, I've been taught, is for those who cherish
goodness over sin:

Near the launch pad at Cape Canaveral,
my sisters and I pose in matching dresses.
At Cypress Gardens we laugh and feed the deer
and on the glass-bottom

boat at Silver Springs, we lean into
Mama, her arms around us. All tenderly
captured in grains of 35mm film,
in these albums painstakingly
chronologized, numbered, my father's work.

It isn't in the photos.
It's in the skimmed over parts,
the never minds and burned letters,
the Cherokee great-grandmother half
acknowledged, in the reason Uncle Norwood
was discharged from the service.
The witnessing too—Grandma's daddy slapping her
in a restaurant in front of me. Granddaddy pushing him down
until the manager intervened and Grandma
stepped in with, *Doc, he ain't never gonna be worth it.*
It's watching her lie down hysterical
behind the Chevy to stop Granddaddy
from leaving one New Year's Day after a fight.

This puzzle lore assembled
becomes the Polish sailor Aunt Deebie married
then abandoned when he was out at sea.
A missing piece: the reason
Uncle Edward laid out newspaper
before he shot himself, hours after the police questioned him.
Uncle Seward's stuttering, Uncle Joe's moonshining,
Aunt Lela and her men. And all those things I can't
even mention because of the hurt to those still living.
My own secrets, conveniently misplaced.

It's all catastrophe.
The death of moments.
A way of life passed on and buried.
Our certain death no matter how
alive the hydrangea bushes appear,
how shiny the 1950 Buick.

Look here—the photo of Granddaddy, Daddy and me,
down by the river. Each of us the last of our generation.
The sundress I wear Grandma made
from towels that came free with laundry soap.
The fossilized shark's tooth I hold, big as my face, dredging
equipment just visible behind us from where they
were deepening the channel. But my eyes squeeze
against the sun, unaware of the wound behind me.
Granddaddy and Daddy hold hands, fingers clenched
so tight the veins run up their forearms, their smiles
an extension of the grip,
their eyes suffering something beyond the lens.

As if I took a razor to my own flesh,
I feel the cut, I feel the pressure
they apply to hold back. To hold back
what?

6. Songs at My Father's Funeral, 1998

Cousins far removed, the great-
Aunts, uncles, grandparents,
Generations of dresses,
Hats, shined-up shoes
And costume jewelry. I let
Them bathe me in the hot air
Flutter of their paper fans.
Tom, Tassie, Kitty, El,

Lela, Nannie Jane, Seward,
Gladys, Solomon, Norwood,
Green Bell, Elsie, Lot—so many singing
Dead. I smelled the nicotine tips
Of Granddaddy's fingers,
Imponderable hand stroking
Their voices into my head.
>   (*Oh, just think*
>   *how in death you will feel,*
>   *with the light growing dim*
>   *in your soul. Oh how long it will be,*
>   *oh how still.*)
The world faded then
His casket lowered—grass and sky,
My own complexion
Ashen too.
The end of the line,
Last of the Youmans males.
Oh how great
Their disappointment must have been
When I slipped
Into this life.
>   (*Life's story for you has been*
>   *told. What a dread*
>   *in your life you would feel.*
>   *When the light has gone out in your soul.*)
Because like my father, I can tell
You what's in a name: Deeds,
Telegrams, Expired Driver's
Licenses, Birth, Baptismal,
Wedding, Death
Certificates, Encumbrances
Preserved in box
>   (*Will you miss me?*)

After box:
GM Mechanic's Exam,
Business Licenses, Letters, Tenant Farm
Agreements, Gun
Permits, Photographs, Newspaper
Clippings, Pink Slips,
Army Discharge Papers,
A passed-on history
                    (*Will you miss me when I'm gone?*)
Hardly worth
Saving I care so much about.
                    (*Perhaps you'll plant a flower on my poor
                    unworthy grave. Come and sit
                    alone beside me
                    when the roses nod and wave.*)
I've eaten the soil we grew
Out of, lain down on
The graves. I've learned
Names, faces of those
Long dead and their stories
Have fixed on me an impenetrable gaze
I can't shake—my father's sadness
That he left nothing for the world
To remember him by.

III

When before the judgment bar you shall stand

And your deeds of your life have been told,

Good and Evil appears so what then?

—A. P. Carter

What if I stopped
questioning the Resurrection.
Stopped desiring
proof in the shroud, modern hands mystically impaled

and bloody. No longer looked to the fold
in my kitchen curtains, the mottled linoleum floor,
staring so hard the beard becomes visible.
Those lamenting eyes.

If I no longer second guessed the Holy Ghost,
the way it rushes in, diffuses the body,
emerges through unimmaculate mouths,
perhaps my soul would get unclogged.

Who am I anyway?
I am afraid
to tell you. What I believe
isn't enlightened.

Some days I lift my
arms and sky spills out
of my hands. Others, I look down at
the words and see nothing in between.

The House of My Mother's Shame

Creep too near the house of my mother's shame
and I'll draw the curtains quick!
I won't supply you with details and names,

though most have died their little deaths, to blame
the dust for being dirty doesn't get rid of it.
I sweep the house of my mother's shame,

then burn the refuse and study the flames
that threaten these poor white rooms—who gives a shit
about the squalid details, the no-account names.

My vigilance is wasted here. The past a freeze-frame
of averted eyes. I bore through photos of the dead and sick,
their closed mouths full of details and names.

I pass through these rooms dismissing claims
of chatty born-again ghosts. Salvation, their last trick,
pulled off in the house of my mother's shame.

In my worst dream, my whole body is a stain,
a birthmark curse for the kindred heretic.
I am the house of my mother's shame.
I could supply you with details and names.

Late at night after rain is best, soil loose
as pudding. You can kneel among rows

of pole beans, rutabagas, prize-winning
azaleas and mock orange shrubs.

Like a tea party with heirloom silver and blue
willow bowls or a family reunion

with Tupperware and throwaway spoons,
as if it were no different

than devouring tomatoes
right off the vine, you eat the dirt.

Pregnant women, wiping blackened mouths
with the backs of hands believe babies

will slip out slick as seals and free
of birthmarks. Satin robed wives

wearing diamond rings sneak from their beds, hungry
for the corner of the yard belonging solely to them—

beneath the magnolia where nothing will grow,
the only spot that hasn't been fertilized,

manicured by husbands who find such comfort
purveying their even seas of green. And standing

fixed in the soil, nightgown flapping on her worn
body like laundry left on the line,

the widow with sterling-blue hair digs
a hole until her fingers bruise from dirt

crammed behind her nails, knees
stiff and hurt from kneeling down

too long. Spoons and china forgotten,
she gorges, dirt covering the front of her

gown, caking her arms and chest. She does this
until her stomach aches and swells and she lies

there humming songs—
"Apple Blossom Time," "Red River Valley."

I said I don't know who put the fruit salad
in Aunt Mildred's purse. *Ambrosia*
Mama corrected, as if through the name
brown fruit, marshmallows, coconut, sour

cream became something more.
Why it showed up at every family reunion
floating on tired lettuce, I couldn't tell you.
Aunt Ater didn't want it on her plate,

she wanted chocolate cake. But no one
asked her as she sat rocking on her porch,
spitting snuff into the green
Folger's coffee can. *Ping*—tinny and clear

resonated in the sweet gum trees
and in my ears, while relatives nosed
through her rooms for some memory,
some piece of themselves they left or forgot.

Of course, they greeted her, making their way
up the bowed steps, bearing smells of okra,
squash casserole, ambrosia—always
polite, saying things like, *Oh Aunt Ater*

you're pretty as a picture sitting there.
But I looked at her cataract clouded eyes,
gray hair coarse and thick as the bristles
on a razorback boar. I saw her

lips slip past her gums as she smiled,
waved at their passing. How can she eat
the apples without her teeth? They were misplaced
weeks ago. But Aunt Mildred had cousins

to tend to. I took the plate from Aunt Ater
and gave her cake on a napkin. I ran my hand over her
wire hair and kissed her cup-shaped cheek. She ate it
then asked for seconds. I tell you she wanted more.

If I knew which veins carried Hampton blood,
I'd slice them all wide open.

—Grandma Alease Hampton Youmans

She said her daddy was cruel.
I don't know the many ways.
I have my own ideas—how cold
the winters got,
how small the house. How
a body made her shiver.

She said a coral snake once wrapped
itself around her wrist like a
cloisonné bracelet. It was
important to be still.
I asked her why she spent
her childhood summers beneath
the porch. I asked her why
she wasn't afraid there.
Red and yellow, kill a fellow.
Red and black, nice to Jack.
Remember that, she said.

In fall, beneath the arborvitae
dropped needles poked her
skin like tiny bayonets.
She'd stay there for hours,
rigid as a two-by-four.
Anyone could walk all over her
she said—she wouldn't feel a thing.
Injecting insulin into her thigh,
she didn't even flinch.

Aunt Kitty Walks Out,
or The Magician's Assistant Quits the Act

What follows gives me away,
My lack of guile and going it alone.
In bed I chew my nails, your obvious toupee,
They give me strength of teeth and bone.

No fear of heights I have or depths,
The tide lifts up, the sky throws back.
But I look down and count each step
To ward off demons. I've seen their tracks.

Give back what you stole from me,
The few dimes, stray hairs and my pink barrette,
A glossy photo of some dark brute, three
Times I've asked and the spell is left

Unbroken. I do not move as others do, I saw
Myself in half. Oh the way flesh mends and grows!
A ravine revolts inside of me, entrails crawl
Like tropic vines and azaleas crowd my heart out, slow

Me down on cold March days. About the severed
Let us not speak, nor my carelessness. Who took
My warmth but you? Reel and reel, but I was never
Caught. I saw the worm. I saw the hook.

Antinomian Apostrophe

At night
sometimes
my breath
comes in quick
gasps. Squeeze
of many
fingers around
my neck.

I've been on
the other
side, crushed
a windpipe
like a pretzel.
What can
I tell you?

I'm guilty
of so much
it seems.
But you
are worse
off than me.

There are red-
hot pinchers
seething in coals
because
you've not
been picked.

I took the blame
when silver
mold swallowed

the neighbor's
berries. I pulled out
my eyelashes one
by one. But I
carry spiders
back outside.

The odds
needn't be
tilted in
my favor.
It's all bonus,
like waving
people into traffic
when the right
of way is mine.
Divine grace
like black
leather gloves
fits me.
But you,
Brother,
you don't
have a prayer.

Language of Angels, Prophets
and even Saint Paul of Tarsus,

full of the Holy Ghost. I had faith
in Aunt Sula, though no one else did.

Especially Daddy thought she was full
of herself and the devil. *You can't test God*

he'd say as she slipped strychnine
into her tea like sugar. Sometimes

she knelt down in front of me, and washed
my feet. She looked up at me and spoke

through lips still swollen with glossolalia.
Just like Christ did for his disciples. I believed

in her and the pure whiteness
of her hands, rose painted nails,

skin soft as the silk dresses
she wore, unmarked

by the snakes that bit
while she caressed them.

My Mother Tells Me Stories

She says it would be awful
except she likes being alone, the quiet
house. No CNN, no oxygen
machine drone, no death rattle trapped
inside my father's chest.
I suggest perhaps it isn't the
aloneness, but the relief
from vigilance. She tells me working
in the yard as long as she wants is nice.

I ask if she's very hungry these days. She tells
me she never understood how he could
eat chicken-a-la-king from a can. Or how,
at the end, he thought Winn Dixie's bottled sweet tea
tasted better than her own.
Her gravy either too runny or too thick,
never like his Mama made.

She mentions that she's singing
in the choir again. I ask about the church
I grew up in, who she sees.
Atlantic Boulevard is so busy, she says, it
takes twenty minutes to get there
when it used to take ten.

I want to know if she cries
or if she ever goes to the cemetery
or if she's forgotten all those years
he wasn't sick, the way I sometimes think I have.

Last afternoon I pulled weeds
from the bed of impatiens, she tells me,
and I saw a cat nestled there.
I pet it, and it was an armadillo.

The darndest thing the way it stayed
there letting me stroke its stony hide.

Dissipation

Even snakes tremble in this land of trembling
earth, where cloaked in the Okefenokee

a man stands on an alligator's back and prays
it is a dream. His or another's.

He knows, a foot lifts off—a heel strays a bit
and the stupefied is supper. The alligator

doesn't move a breath and the man wonders
if he's sleeping. It doesn't matter, the hand's

been dealt, an alligator's eyelids are windows
and the man wears an alligator belt.

Frogs' throated dirge, the whir
and thrum of insects quarrel in

the man's ears, beat his drums until he's
dizzy. It's curious, his thoughts don't run

to a wife, grandbabies, what's left undone.
Instead he thinks of alligators

that climb ladders then swoosh belly down
a slide, one after another, glide into a pool

at a roadside reptile playground. Eyes
devoid of joy, despite the frolic. Like exotic

dancers, the man remembers. It's best
to ignore their gaze, sluggish and bored.

Focus on the skin—a smooth, taut belly
beneath your hands is worth something:

A sin kept from your snoring wife,
a pair of alligator boots. There is

little good in life, the man decides. Bubbles rise
from the snout submerged and as they burst

he hears the alligator croon, *It's all
been wasted, down to now. The closest you'll*

*ever get to true. Not a lick
of help here for what ails you.*

Beneath stars he doesn't risk looking up to see,
the man's stomach growls and the pied

didapper wails back its own need.
The man wishes the moon

was brighter, that he'd worn a heavier shirt.
He wishes it wasn't already September,

that his knees didn't hurt so much.
The man wishes and he wishes and he winces and he wishes.

The Anole

slinks
among the stepping
   stones while all the grass between measures
   his domain like a map drawn
      vigilant with boundaries. Green as

bottle
glass, he expects
   he isn't seen camouflaged so
   capably in lawn. One eye blinks,
      queries me and the other waits

patient
as a widow
   for crickets hush-hidden
   in the soil. I move
      closer. He stays, still

certain
of the guise.
   His skin, all verdancy and mood,
   breathes (I can almost *see*
      it the grass trembles

about
him). Scales
   yielding as worn leather appeal to
   me to touch, to hold
      him for something close to

luck
or better.
   My fingertips graze over
   his head, back,
      and this air around him

groans.
Up and down
   his body convulses, his dewlap red
   like contagion extends, strong-
      armed he seems to grow larger and larger

before
me. It's just
   a moment then only his tail,
   salience and charm,
      remains shuddering on the stone.

Empires

What is there left to offer up?
Enough squirrels, mice, blue jays, headless
rabbits left at the door—dear cat who
strives to please. The carnage I am
responsible for unnerves me,
so I do not keep count. I've never been good
with numbers. These days even fractions
disturb me, the severing of figures.
If it's whole what should be taken away?
A foot, a tail, a heart (I think that's a heart),
bits of fur and feathers.
I am a believer and am not afraid
of being dead—only the period of suffering before.
Any prize worth having demands some sacrifice
of time and energy, I suppose. But daily
I feel sadness over the passing of others.
The last breath, the last molecule of breath. Though
stray hairs may still be found months later on
December's gray coat and molted skin cells
abound in every room, these were
already lifeless and collected are only relics.
So much small dead.
Today it is a blue jay (I imagine their squawking
annoys him), and comfortable in rule, Louie lies on
the patio table, shielded by an umbrella, flourishing
his tail like a flag. An aviary U.N. convokes,
shrieking grievances, but never rush at him.
Through French doors I watch the world
at work. I am not God and do not know
my cat's mind. I scarcely know my own,
but in my heart are four small rooms and that
is where I live. In two chambers are saints

and in the other two are demons. With the first I am all
soul, and the second, merely flesh. Sitting with evil,
the egos revolt me, but the near-perfect make me
unworthy of my own pulse.
I am tedious and walk the hall that separates these
rooms, so I'll never amount to much.
I do not wish to take over the world,
nor do I think I can save it.

R-E-V-E-L-A-T-I-O-N TEN letters—TEN commandments—both
GOD'S WARNING
For SINNERS! MATTHEW
                    MARK
                    LUKE
                    JOHN!
While Mama made fig jam,
I licked the spoon out in the yard
And watched Aunt Ater go.
Knotted fingers thumping her thighs,
She gawked bald-eyed at the sun.
FOUR Gospels—FOUR
Horsemen—four BEASTS in CHAPTER FOUR.
Holy. Holy. Holy.
Louder each time she yelled
My shoulders jumped. The veins
On her calves bulged and quivered,
Her blood was boiling—I thought
If I touched the hem of her dress
We could all go up in flames.
Lord GOD ALMIGHTY
Which WAS and IS and IS to come.
G-E-N-E-S-I-S—seven letters—SEVEN DAYS GOD
Created EARTH.
                    SEVEN archangels—Seventh
Seal means DEATH to them UNSAVED!
Squinting my eyes like a newborn,
I stood behind her stunned by all
The glare, by all the ants.
One hundred ants marching up my leg.

Bacon grease, teaberry gum—even his Bible
smelled like him. Not just
a Sunday supplement, but fixed
to his hand all week long, sewn
with Heaven's golden thread. *A m-m-m-*
mailman ain't n-nothing withhhhout the mail.

Uncle Seward stuttered. But off
his tongue gospel rolled like bones.
Sometimes he let me throw the dice when no one
was around. His moth-wing eyelids
fluttered, implored the kitchen
light—would Granddaddy Hamp stop
drinking, Petie find Jesus,
Lela's leg b-b-be rrransomed
of Satan's c-c-c-cancer? I'd pitch
across the table.

The rest was up to God, Uncle Seward
only did what he was told—how
many dice to read, Old
Testament or New. One hand
covering his eyes, while his finger
like a compass needle carried out
the prophecy. Once, just like that,
I rolled 6-6-6. *It don't mean n-n-nothing,*
but he fumbled through the onionskin
pages while I held my breath.
His voice like mercury, silver
and fluid fever rose above my head:

Behold, the whirlwind of the Lord goeth forth
with fury, a continuing whirlwind: it shall
fall with pain upon the head of the wicked.

I waited for a can of Vienna sausages
to fly across the room, or hear
laughter rumble up through the floor.
I mean I was sore afraid.

With one hundred angels perched upon your shoulders. Still you'd
keep your own guard.

Even a voice, resounding certain as a doorbell in my heart, rouses
questions of heaven or hell.

The devil is in your mind, therefore he is with you always.

Not evil's disembodied tongue. I want salvation to hurl me like a
brick through doubt's dingy window.

Around and through you, God moves like the ponderous air.

A breath. A hurricane. I believe.

He can stroke the wings of a fly without breaking them.

Help me with my disbelief.

Why do you let the world impose its will?

The devil is in my mind, therefore he is with me always.

Why do you let the world impose its will?

I haven't suffered as I should.
I haven't suffered enough.

Hellebore

Through the frozen earth hellebore emerges,
a Lenten rose crusted over with snow.
The forgiving sun through its leaves surges
down toward roots tingling with no

sense as to why, but they comply unquestioning.
Inside the crush-buried bloom, lush leaves, poison stirs
out of habit, like an annoying tune we sing
anyway. It cannot shun its nature.

No memory of storm and drought. No memory of wind.
Hellebore won't restrain itself from fear
of failure, lackluster grace. Everyday we offend
without meaning to offend. Let us hear

beyond the rise and fall of our own beating hearts.
Let us find our way feelingly upward through the dark.

Teri Youmans Grimm has taught in the Writer's Workshop at the University of Nebraska, Omaha. She is an editor-at-large for Zoo Press. Her writing has appeared in the *Connecticut Review*, *Indiana Review*, *Prairie Schooner*, *The Journal*, *Columbia: A Journal of Literature and Art*, and other publications.

Photo by Chad Grimm